I believe in you

First Edition
20 19 18 17 16   5 4 3 2 1

Text © 2016 Gibbs Smith
Illustrations © 2016 Gibbs Smith

Published by
Gibbs Smith
P.O. Box 667
Layton, Utah 84041

1.800.835.4993 orders
www.gibbs-smith.com

Designed by Sky Hatter

Printed and bound in Hong Kong

Gibbs Smith books are printed on either recycled, 100% post-consumer waste, FSC-certified papers or on paper produced from sustainable PEFC-certified forest/controlled wood source. Learn more at www.pefc.org.

Library of Congress Cataloging-in-Publication Data
Library of Congress Control Number: 2016930183
ISBN: 9781423644804

I believe in you

Illustrated by Sky Hatter

GIBBS SMITH
TO ENRICH AND INSPIRE HUMANKIND

Chapter 1

SPOILER ALERT: Everything is going to be FINE!

She believed she could,

so she did.

—R.S. Grey

It looks good on you.

Be somebody's

sunshine today.

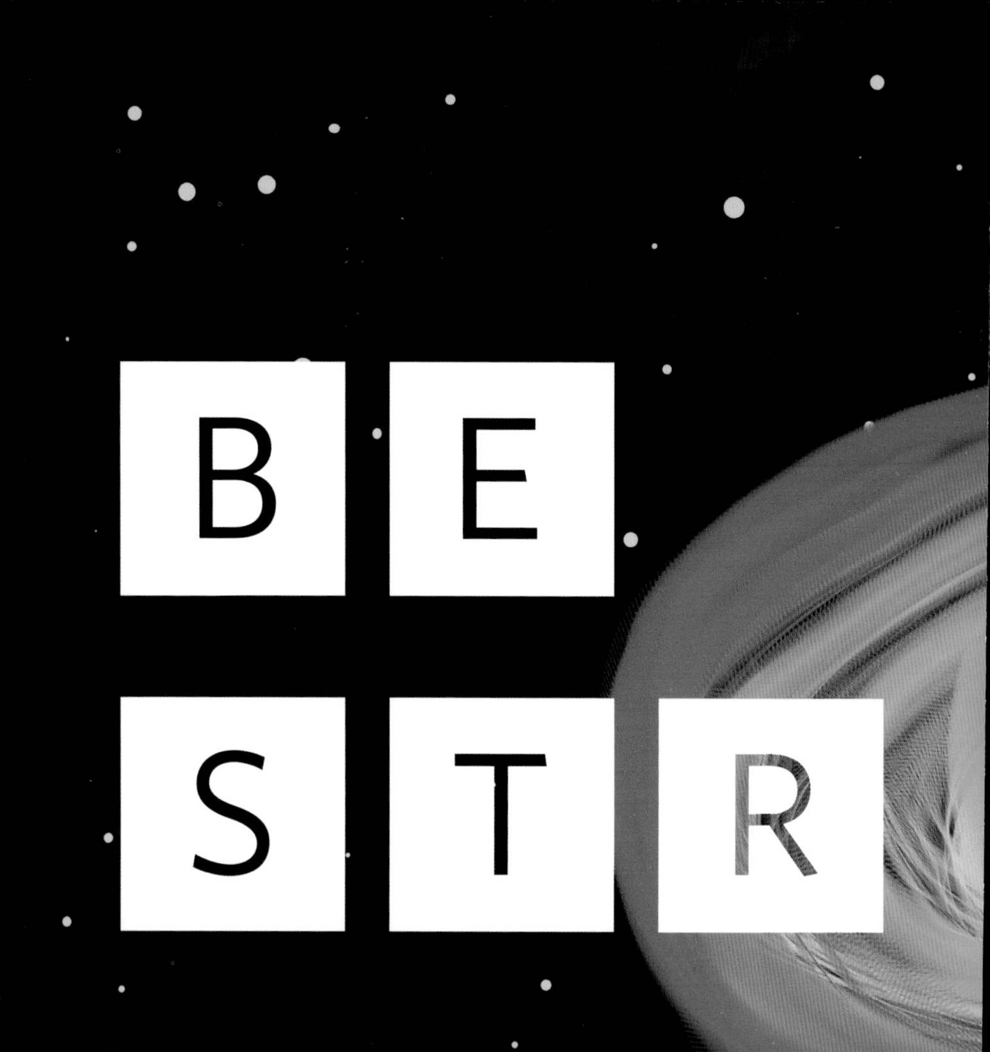
B E
S T R

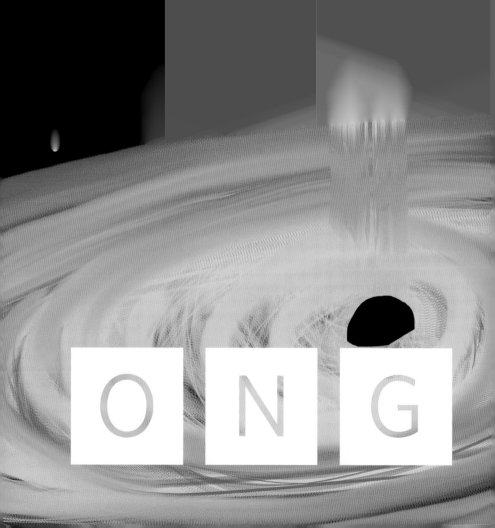

IT'S
OK

When you
come to the end of your
rope,
tie a knot and hang on.

NEVER COMPARE YOUR BEGINNING

TO SOMEONE ELSE'S MIDDLE.

—Jon Acuff

I AM YOUR BIGGEST FAN.

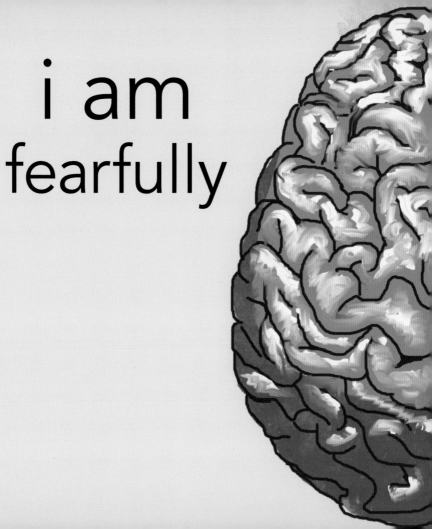

i am
fearfully

and
WONDERFULLY
MADE

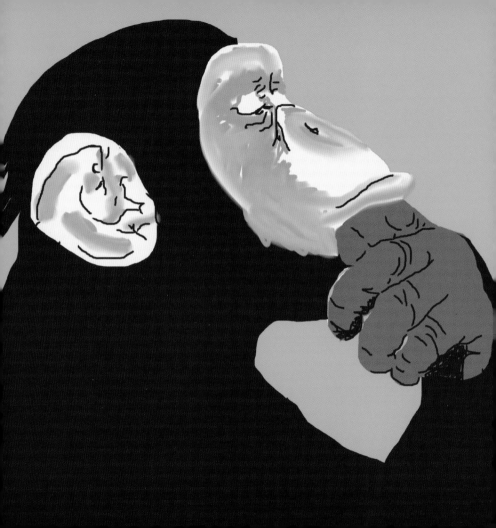

THINK GOOD THOUGHTS

GOOD THINGS

are going to
happen today.

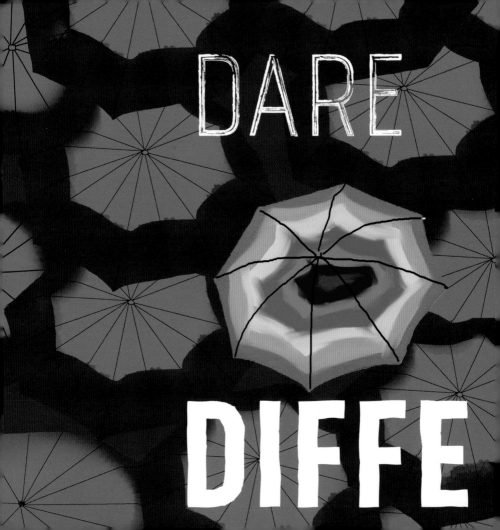

Make some
lemonade.

We cannot direct the wind,
but we can adjust the sails.

— Thomas S. Monson

I believe in you.

NG

IN THERE

Always be
yourself.*

*Unless you can be a unicorn, then always be a unicorn.

YOU NEED

DEEP IN

BEFORE

YOUR

TO BE BURIED

THE DIRT

YOU CAN FIND

BLOOM.

—ROZ INGA

CHASE YOUR DREAMS

LIFE IS BETTER
with friends.

IT'S NOT WHETHER YOU GET KNOCKED DOWN,

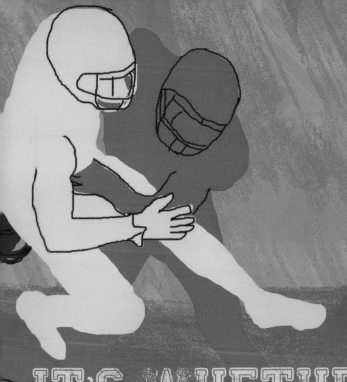

IT'S WHETHER YOU GET UP.

—Vince Lombardi

Reach as high as you can,
and then reach a little higher.

There you will find magic
and possibility. And maybe
even cookies.

—Marc Johns

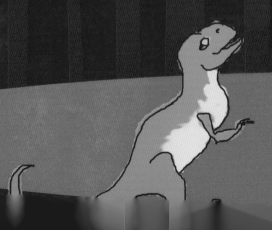

SUCCESS

comes in

CANS

not can'ts

Just when the caterpillar thought the world was over,

it became a
butterfly.

WHEN IT IS DARK ENOUGH,

YOU CAN SEE STARS.

—*Ralph Waldo Emerson*

A woman is like a tea bag.

You never know how strong she is until you put her in hot water.

Life is like riding

To keep your

balance,

you must keep

a bicycle.

noving.

—Albert Einstein

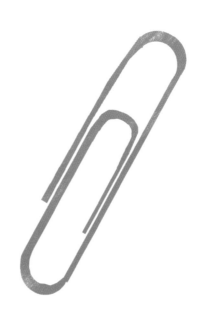

Do what
you **CAN**,
with what
you've **GOT**,
WHERE
you are.

–Squire Bill Widener

THE TRUTH WILL SET YOU FREE,

but first it will piss you off.

—Gloria Steinem

POUR YOURSELF A
drink,
PUT ON SOME
lipstick,
AND PULL YOURSELF
together.

—ELIZABETH TAYLOR

Let your soul stand cool and composed before a million universes.

–Walt Whitman

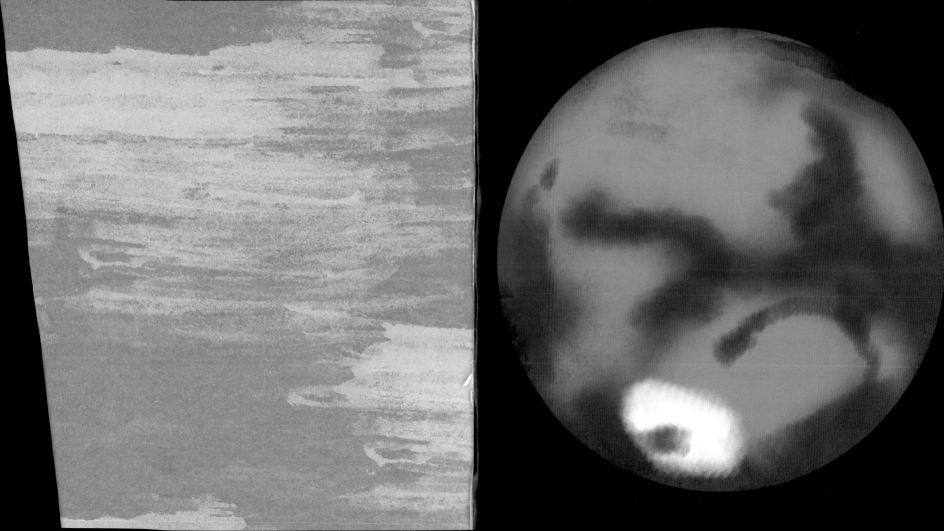

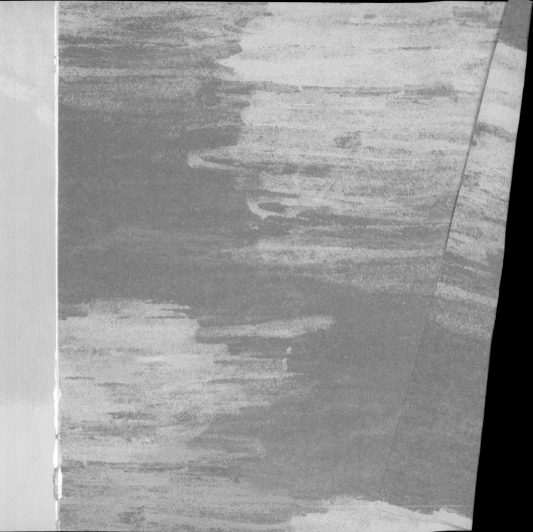

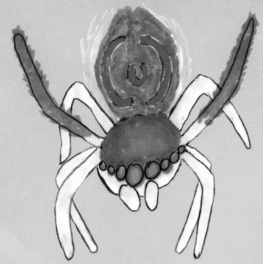

The things that make you

DIFFERENT

are the things that

MAKE YOU

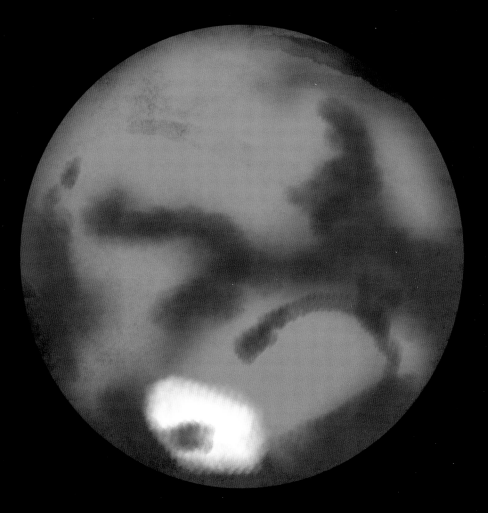

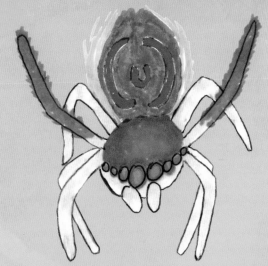

The things that make you

DIFFERENT

are the things that

MAKE YOU